# Jesus is the Real Power

## (Not Magic)

By Peyton Gober

©2008

Parson's Porch Books

*Jesus is the Real Power (Not Magic)*
ISBN: Softcover 978-1-955581-77-6
Copyright © 2022 by Peyton Gober

**Special thanks to Dottie Bradley for her illustrations on the cover and throughout the book.**

**Parson's Porch Books** is an imprint of Parson's Porch & Company (PP&C) in Cleveland, Tennessee. PP&C is an innovative organization which raises money by publishing books of noted authors, representing all genres. Its face and voice is **David Russell Tullock** (dtullock@parsonsporch.com).

Parson's Porch & Company *turns books into bread & milk* by sharing its profits with the poor.

www.parsonsporch.com

# INTRODUCTION

It was just an ordinary day of a grandmother helping a grandchild clean her room. I was in Birmingham visiting my son's family and my granddaughter, Peyton, wanted (well, maybe she was encouraged) to clean out her closet. It was early in the summer after her third-grade school year. The closet floor was piled high with clothes, shoes, and school "stuff" all the way up to her hanging clothes! I told her everything had to come out of the closet and then we would sort, throw away, and reorganize before putting it back. When we began to see the floor at the very bottom of the pile, I noticed some schoolwork that looked interesting with the title "Jesus is the Real Power (Not Magic)" in Peyton's handwriting. I picked it up and was immediately mesmerized at this child-made book stapled together.

I said, "Peyton, what is this?"

Peyton very casually looked over and said "Oh… it's a book I wrote last year".

It certainly did not have the appearance of a casual book a typical 8-year-old would write in public school. I think I knew right then that it was special, so I said, "Go put this beside my bed in the guest room and I will have time to read it this afternoon."

After a few more questions, I learned that Peyton's teacher had assigned the students a book writing project where students could write about any topic. Peyton chose to write about the Trinity, but she also included her belief about Satan and about heaven.

After reading her book later that day…as a teacher myself … I knew that the magnitude of Peyton's understanding of God, Jesus and the Holy Spirit was advanced for her age. I continue even now to be amazed that an eight-year-old child grasped "God in three persons" ...as many adults still struggle with that concept today as mature Christians.

Since that summer day, in 2008, I have shown Peyton's book to many ministers and all of them have told me that her eight-year-old understanding of the Trinity was more advanced than many of their church members. Sometimes a child can show us a simple way of understanding something that appears to be complex. In the New Testament, I believe Jesus does the same.

I also believe Peyton's writing is an example of what can happen when parents intentionally talk with their children about God. Because of strong Christian parents, she "gets it" thanks to their teaching of "the most important life lesson" as Peyton says in her dedication. I have no doubt that Peyton's church leaders/teachers/ministers also played a part in her understanding of this important concept.

WHAT THIS BOOK IS NOT:

• It is not intended to be a bragging book about my grandchild.

• It is not intended to put Peyton or her parents on a pedestal that they are "better" or "wiser" than any other parents.

WHAT THIS BOOK IS:

• It is intended to help the reader have a better understanding of "God in three persons".

• It is intended to show the influence Christian parents can have with their children if they talk openly and honestly at an early age about Biblical truths/concepts/scripture and more.

• It is intended to show that even Biblical truths (as the Trinity) can be discussed in simple, child-like terms as Peyton shows us here. When children grow up with conversations in their home (as well as in church) about God starting at an early age, the concepts can stay with them into adulthood.

• It is intended to be read/discussed by children, parents, Sunday School teachers, youth directors, youth groups, and ministers. Both children and adults of any age will enjoy and benefit from Peyton's story.

Why publish Peyton's story 14 years after she wrote it? I have asked myself that question for many years as I have thought about having it published but did not pursue it. God has continued to talk to me about finding a way to share it, so I decided to honor His will. It must be part of God's plan as He led me to Parson's Porch and David Tullock. Thank you, David, for your vision as well as your help and encouragement as you have created the publishing avenue for authors like Peyton.

So...here is Peyton's book, complete with her own titles, unique third grade spelling, her own handwriting and her simple explanation of God, Jesus, and the Holy Spirit. Please be aware that there are some statements in the book that are not entirely accurate, but they represent an 8-year old's thinking and do not take away from the true meaning.

I hope the book brings you as much joy as it has brought me over the last 14 years. My only regret is waiting so long to share her story.

**Sue Gober, Ed.D.,** taught kindergarten for many years and then trained early childhood teachers at the college level. She retired in 2016 as Professor from the School of Education at the University of Mobile. She is Peyton's grandmother and she and Peyton would love to hear from you. She can be reached at suegober@gmail.com.

Deticated to my parents who have taught me all that you are about to read. I love you. Thank you so much for teaching me the most important life lesson there is.

# Introduction

Dear readers,

This story you are about to read is not only a really, very, the most important life lesson, but it is true. I hope you enjoy this book.

Flip the page to begin.

# Chapter One

## About Jesus

Most people think that Jesus is just a made up story. Or a legend that was made up years ago, and is still being told today. And some kind of believe, but just ignore it an worship other fake gods.

If you are at all questioning Him being the only way all you have to do is read a little bit of the bible. A certin part. I'm not sur what part but you can always try. If you read the right part, it will teach you that the same Jesus that was alive millions of years ago, is the same Jesus thay we pay to today. And He will be forever. And he is the power. Unlike Kings, Queens, or Satin He rules everything. I mean think about Kings and Queens, When they die, new people take there place. Jesus was, is, and will always be the same person. Satin will, too. But he dosn't rule over anything

He tries to get hold of your mind, and make you do bad things, have bad action and set poor exaples for others. Just remember to always be a Christ follower.

# Chapter two
# the Holy spirit

The holy spirit is something that is inside of you. Sometimes you might hear people say that God has three heads. It's true! God dosn't litteraly have three heads, but, what people mean is that you' have:

- God
- Jesus
- Holy spirt

Holy Spirit

He lives inside your heart.

The holy spirit is the form of god that lives inside of you. It's that little voice inside that when you are temp d to do the wrong thing, it is tel ling you to do the right thing.

So whenever you hear the little voice telling you to do the right thing, do what it says, and you will have a much better life than if you always did the wrong thing and got punished all of the time. The Holy Spirit went into action when Jesus went to heaven.

# Chapter three

# Satin

Satin is the one who always wants you to do the wrong thing. He's that other little voice that is telling You to do the wrong thing

# DON'T LISTEN!

And I mean it. That loud and clear Because he is the one who always wants you to do the wrong thing, lik I said. Like I said earlier, if you do you will get in trouble all of the time and your life will be misarable. You don't want to live your life misarable do you? No way!! All you have to do is simply don't listen!

# Chapter Four

## Jesus is the Only Way

If you have Jesus in your heart, you
will go to Heavyn. And Heavyn is wonderful
There is no sin in Heavyn! No getting
hurt.etheir! I don't know about you
but I want to go to Heavyn. But
you can't go because you want to.
you do it for the right reason.

You exept christ to be your lord and Savior. That's all it takes. But do it because the holy spirit told you to. And if you aren't in that state of mind yet and you don't do it. Before asking him to come inside you, and live in you, you might consider Praying! The Holy Spirit might tell you it's not the right time. Then wait, and keep praying. If the Holy spirit says go ahead, then great! Go ahead. But have someone guide you through it!. But overall, you're ready!

The End

CPSIA information can be obtained
at www.ICGtesting.com
Printed in the USA
LVHW070206121022
730384LV00042B/853